D1524452

REAL TEENS... REAL ISSUES

ALCOHOL ABUSE

Katie Marsico

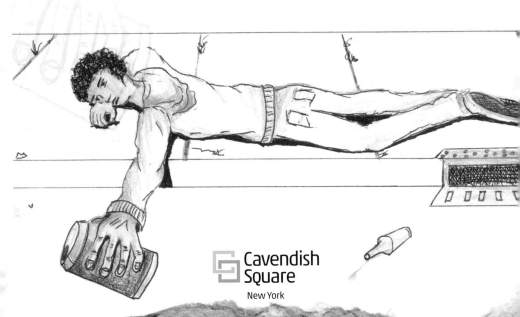

Cavendish
Square
New York

The author would like to dedicate this book to Lynne, Kyle, Josh, Emily, Sandra, William, Brian Bossany, and Claudia Welke, MD. She extends her sincere gratitude to her editor, Christine Florie, whose support and guidance in writing this book proved invaluable.

To protect the privacy of sources, only first names are used throughout the book. Any first names that are asterisked (*) indicate the use of a pseudonym.

Published in 2014 by Cavendish Square Publishing, LLC
303 Park Avenue South, Suite 1247, New York, NY 10010

Copyright © 2014 by Cavendish Square Publishing, LLC

First Edition

Website: cavendishsq.com

This publication represents the opinions and views of the author based on his or her personal experience, knowledge, and research. The information in this book serves as a general guide only. The author and publisher have used their best efforts in preparing this book and disclaim liability rising directly or indirectly from the use and application of this book.

CPSIA Compliance Information: Batch #WS13CSQ

All websites were available and accurate when this book was sent to press.

LIBRARY OF CONGRESS CATALOGING-IN-PUBLICATION DATA
Marsico, Katie, 1980–
Alcohol abuse / Katie Marsico.
p. cm. — (Real teens . . . real issues)
Summary: "Provides comprehensive information on alcohol abuse, including first-person interviews, signs and symptoms, physical dangers, recovery, and solutions"
—Provided by publisher.
Includes bibliographical references and index.
ISBN 978-1-60870-848-2 (hardcover) ISBN 978-1-62712-125-5 (paperback)
ISBN 978-1-60870-854-3 (ebook)
1. Teenagers—Alcohol use—Juvenile literature. 2. Alcoholism—Juvenile literature. 3. Alcohol—Health aspects—Juvenile literature. 4. Alcohol—Physiological literature. I. Title. II. Series.
RJ506.A4M37 2013
618.3_686—dc23
2011029915

EDITOR: Christine Florie
ART DIRECTOR: Anahid Hamparian   SERIES DESIGNER: Kristen Branch

EXPERT READER: John Schulenberg, PhD, Professor, Department of Psychology, Research Professor, Institute for Social Research, University of Michigan, Ann Arbor

Photo research by Marybeth Kavanagh
Title page illustration by Corinne Florie

Printed in the United States of America

CONTENTS

J+K= B.F.F

There are many reasons people drink alcohol. For some individuals, however, drinking can evolve into a cycle of abuse.

ALWAYS DRUNK AND ALMOST DEAD

FOURTEEN-YEAR-OLD LYNNE* RECALLS drinking for the first time at age ten. Both her mother and older brother suffered from alcohol addiction, and it wasn't long before the North Carolina teen experienced similar problems.

STARTLING STAT

ACCORDING TO A 2010 STUDY BY THE INSTITUTE FOR SOCIAL RESEARCH AT THE UNIVERSITY OF MICHIGAN, NEARLY 14 PERCENT OF EIGHTH GRADERS REPORTED THAT THEY DRANK ALCOHOL.

5

"I drank to get drunk," Lynne admits. "I could typically finish one-fifth of a bottle of hard liquor or an entire case of beer. After a while, I also began experimenting with drugs." By the time she turned thirteen, Lynne was regularly drinking to the point of losing consciousness. Yet she continued flooding her young body with alcohol until she gradually realized that this behavior was resulting in more pain than pleasure. "I drank until I was close to death," she reflects. "It made me feel so miserable that I was begging for God to just kill me."

> "I drank until I was close to death. It made me feel so miserable that I was begging for God to just kill me."
> — Lynne

Fortunately, it didn't take death to ease her suffering. Friends and family encouraged her to get help and, terrified of the path she was heading down, Lynne agreed. She began attending **Alcoholics Anonymous (AA)** meetings, which offer group support to people dealing with substance abuse. Though she does admit to still occasionally drinking in moderation, she takes pride in the recovery she has achieved up to this point.

"It's all about finding the willpower to be a different person than I was before, which I am," Lynne reflects. "There's not a day that goes by that I'm not scared of going back to where I was."

AN OVERVIEW OF ALCOHOL ABUSE

Lynne's experiences reveal why alcohol abuse is such a complex and disturbing issue. Unfortunately, it is not a rare one. Yet what exactly does the term "alcohol abuse" mean? According to medical experts, it is important to understand that alcoholism is different from alcohol abuse. Researchers with the National Institutes of Health (NIH) explain this distinction as follows: "*Alcoholism* occurs when a person shows signs of physical addiction to alcohol (e.g. tolerance and withdrawal) and continues to drink, despite problems with physical health, mental health, and social, family, or job responsibilities. Alcohol may come to dominate the person's life and relationships. In *alcohol abuse*, a person's drinking leads to problems, but not physical addiction."

Despite these differences, most experts agree that alcohol abuse can quickly transform into alcoholism. In addition, both conditions have the power to destroy people's lives. Even if someone isn't considered an alcoholic, his or her drinking can result in everything from a fatal car accident to alcohol poisoning to problems with law enforcement officials. So why would a person risk health and happiness to drink?

For starters, many people drink alcoholic beverages to experience the effects they produce when they are absorbed into the bloodstream. Because alcohol is a depressant, it slows down the operation of the nervous system. This causes drinkers to become more relaxed. It also alters, or changes, their emotions, senses, and perceptions.

People who drink occasionally may never struggle with alcohol abuse or alcoholism. Yet some begin to view drinking as their main way to achieve feelings of pleasure or relaxation. They may eventually rely on alcohol so much that it interferes with their personal relationships and overall performance at school, work,

"For a person who abuses alcohol, it's not unusual for their drinking to get out of control—to almost take over their life."
— Brian Bossany

Alcohol abuse can lead to loss of control.

and other areas of day-to-day life. People who abuse alcohol frequently experience these problems.

"For a person who abuses alcohol, it's not unusual for their drinking to get out of control—to almost take over their life," says Brian Bossany, a recovery counselor at Sobriety High. This Minnesota charter-school system provides ninth- to twelfth-grade students with a "safe, sober, and chemical-free environment" where they can attend classes and earn their diplomas.

As Bossany explains, the students he works with generally have one goal in mind when they drink. "I hear . . . a lot of kids say, 'Why bother drinking if you don't drink to get drunk?'" This reflection is evidence that people who abuse alcohol often drink to the point of becoming intoxicated. They may

STARTLING STAT

IN 2010 THE CENTERS FOR DISEASE CONTROL AND PREVENTION (CDC) REPORTED THAT MORE THAN 25 PERCENT OF HIGH SCHOOL STUDENTS ADMITTED TO BINGE DRINKING.

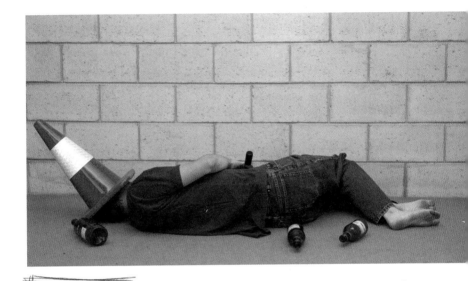

Consuming too much alcohol can cause people to lose consciousness, or pass out.

also binge drink, or consume great amounts of alcohol in a short period of time. These individuals tend to experience blackouts, which occur when they drink so much that they later have no recollection of their behavior. Some make poor or irresponsible choices—including the decision to drive drunk—while under the influence of alcohol.

Since drinking alcohol reduces a driver's reaction time, U.S. laws prohibit anyone with a certain blood alcohol concentration (BAC) from operating

11

a motor vehicle. Police use blood and **Breathalyzer** tests to determine BAC, the grams of alcohol present in 100 milliliters of someone's blood. A driver who is twenty-one or older with a BAC of 0.08 or higher is considered too intoxicated to safely operate a car.

Drunk drivers face many risks, including arrest.

Sadly, being arrested on a charge of driving under the influence of alcohol (DUI) is sometimes not enough to convince a person that he or she has a drinking problem. It is not uncommon for people who abuse alcohol to have difficulty recognizing and admitting that they are in desperate need of help.

THE SCOPE OF A TROUBLING TOPIC

Despite the fact that it is against the law for any-one younger than twenty-one to buy or consume alcohol, evidence shows that underage drinking is not an uncommon occurrence. In 2009 the **Substance Abuse and Mental Health Services Administration** (**SAMHSA**) revealed that there are nearly 11 million underage drinkers in the United States. Not all of these individuals will ultimately abuse alcohol, but experts predict that roughly 3.5 million will.

According to the CDC, more teenagers drink alcohol than smoke tobacco or use commonly abused street and prescription drugs. Researchers with this federal agency also state that "Among youth, . . . alcohol and other drugs [have] been linked to unintentional injuries, physical fights, academic and occupational [work] problems, and illegal behavior." The CDC

13

similarly connects alcohol abuse to liver, heart, and nerve damage, plus a wide variety of mental illnesses.

In addition, experts believe that this problem is at the root of countless other issues that affect teens, including suicide and date rape. Finally, situations involving underage drinking continue to be among the leading causes of death among American teenagers. In an effort to decrease the number of motor vehicle deaths related to alcohol, zero-tolerance laws restrict people younger than twenty-one from driving if they have even faint traces of alcohol in their blood. This means that underage drinkers who are caught behind the wheel with a BAC greater than 0.00—or, in some states, 0.01 or 0.02—can be criminally charged.

Ironically, these laws do little to change the fact that alcohol remains one of the easiest drugs for people to obtain and abuse. Unlike illegal street drugs or prescription medications, alcohol can be purchased at a store by anyone who can prove that he or she is twenty-one. Alternately, many underage drinkers simply sneak beer, wine, or liquor that their parents have purchased. For some, such behavior—which they might initially see as harmless—can become the first steps in a dangerous and destructive cycle of abuse.

According to the Experts

Since Claudia Welke, MD, treats a great number of younger patients, she has developed a few theories about why they tend to be so hard hit by alcohol abuse. Welke is a psychiatrist and the director of Child and Adolescent Psychiatry Training at North Shore University Health System in Highland Park, Illinois. She is also a clinical instructor at the University of Chicago Pritzker School of Medicine in Chicago, Illinois.

"I'm seeing [patients] who are curious about alcohol [at] earlier and earlier [ages]," Welke notes. "Fifth grade is really when the risk begins nowadays. In addition, there's the undeniable component of drinking being a socially acceptable activity." As Welke observes, people often witness adult role models such as parents using alcohol at home. As a result, drinking doesn't always appear to be as dangerous as doing street drugs or even smoking cigarettes.

"[People] whose parents routinely keep alcohol in the liquor cabinet at home or who see adults having a drink at dinner don't necessarily view drinking as bad," she says. "Some parents even buy alcohol for their [children] because they assume that their kids will end up experimenting with it on their own anyway. . . . Certain [individuals] simply don't perceive the same risk of abuse that they probably would with other substances."

TWO

WHY PEOPLE BATTLE THE BOTTLE

EIGHTEEN-YEAR-OLD KYLE DESCRIBES himself as being "pretty much a really good kid" until high school. In fact, the California teen says that he used to encourage his friends and classmates to avoid alcohol. Yet, hurt and angry by his parents' divorce during his freshman year, Kyle now admits that he rebelled against his mother and father by drinking.

When his mother ultimately enrolled him in a new high school, his mood and overall attitude toward life took a turn for the worse. He remembers feeling like everyone hated him and confesses that it was common for him to become involved in fights with his classmates. In addition, Kyle started

STARTLING STAT

A 2011 CBS NEWS REPORT INDICATED THAT 71 PERCENT OF AMERICANS TRY DRINKING BEFORE THEY FINISH HIGH SCHOOL.

drinking more heavily—sometimes finishing an entire bottle of vodka at parties.

"I wouldn't describe myself [as an alcoholic]," he explains. "I thought I was happy and, when I was drunk, life seemed better. Ultimately, though, I still woke up with the same set of problems every morning."

In reality, Kyle's problems actually worsened as a result of his alcohol abuse. During his sophomore year, his drinking led to run-ins with school and law-enforcement officials. Fortunately, Kyle and his family sought out treatment options that helped him work on getting and staying sober. In fall 2009 he enrolled in a sobriety high school that allowed him to both focus on his recovery and work toward earning his diploma. Two years later, Kyle says he is a different person.

"When I was getting drunk all the time, I feel like I was using one eye to look at life through a straight, narrow pipe. Now I have a much more open view of the world and can see a future ahead of me." — Kyle

"My perspective has definitely changed for the better," he reflects. "When I was getting drunk all the time, I feel like I was using one eye to look at life through a straight, narrow pipe. Now I have a much more open view of the world and can see a future ahead of me."

FINDING COMMON RISK FACTORS

Alcohol abuse affects people of all ages, races, and economic and social backgrounds. Research shows that it is more common in men than women, but there is little doubt that this issue has a negative impact on both genders.

Medical professionals and addiction experts agree that alcohol abuse is a far-reaching problem that controls the lives of millions of Americans. Yet they also recognize that the younger people are when they start

Alcohol abuse is not exclusive to either gender.

drinking, the greater the odds that they will struggle with serious abuse and dependency. Researchers have therefore tried to identify what puts a person at greater risk of abusing alcohol.

One factor is a family history of substance abuse. Someone who has a parent or immediate family member who is suffering from a drinking problem is more likely to experience similar issues. In some cases, a **traumatic**, life-changing event such as death or parental divorce can trigger an emotional disturbance, which, in turn, raises a person's risk of abusing alcohol. Undergoing physical, verbal, or sexual abuse increases these odds as well.

In addition, experts suspect that underage drinkers who can easily access alcohol in their homes or at friends' houses have a heightened risk of developing a drinking problem. They also believe that people who enjoy less open communication with their parents about abusing alcohol face increased odds of suffering from this condition.

Yet family life isn't the only factor that determines people's risk of developing a drinking problem. People dealing with various **comorbid** conditions frequently have a greater likelihood of abusing alcohol. Struggling with depression, stress, eating disorders, and certain learning disabilities all add to this risk.

STARTLING STAT

THE NATIONAL SURVEY ON DRUG USE AND HEALTH (NSDUH) RECENTLY REPORTED THAT ROUGHLY 21 PERCENT OF TEENS SUFFERING FROM SEVERE DEPRESSION WERE ALSO STRUGGLING WITH SUBSTANCE ABUSE.

Research shows that people who struggle with depression have a greater risk of abusing alcohol.

No matter what triggers alcohol abuse, it is common for sufferers to initially be unaware that they have a problem. Some people experience a strong sense of denial about the impact that drinking has on their lives. Unfortunately, the longer they use this attitude to excuse their behavior, the deeper they fall into a cycle of alcohol abuse and dependency.

RECOGNIZING RED FLAGS OF ALCOHOL ABUSE

Just as there are many factors that can lead people to develop a drinking problem, there are also multiple warning signs that alcohol abuse might be occurring. For example, someone who is abusing alcohol may stop fulfilling his or her responsibilities at school, work, and home. Certain individuals display a sudden lack of interest in activities or accomplishments that once gave them pleasure. They may demonstrate a dramatic slip in grades or unexplained changes in athletic performance.

In addition, people who are struggling with alcohol abuse frequently detach themselves from healthy, long-term relationships. They may instead start spending more time with new friends or acquaintances who are known to drink regularly or have access to alcohol.

There are also various physical clues that may hint at alcohol abuse. Some people become less attentive to their overall appearance and personal hygiene. Individuals who are frequently suffering from **hangovers** following periods of heavy drinking may be clearly exhausted, nauseous, and smell like alcohol.

Drinking too much alcohol can trigger feelings of nausea.

Avoid Assumptions!

If friends and family members suspect someone they care about is struggling with alcohol abuse, Claudia Welke recommends that they take action. Assuming that a drinking problem doesn't exist because there aren't obvious warning signs can be a deadly mistake.

"The physical red flags aren't always there if you're looking at [someone] who's abusing alcohol," she notes. "A clearer, more consistent sign is that the person keeps suffering negative consequences because of their drinking—but continues drinking anyway."

They might complain of dizziness or changes in sleep patterns and energy levels. Many people who abuse alcohol exhibit unexplained shifts in appetite and weight. They may also appear to have glassy, bloodshot eyes. In addition, they might talk about experiencing headaches and ongoing respiratory symptoms, including a runny nose and sore throat.

More drastic physical signs that point to alcohol abuse are injuries that result from accidents, fights, or motor vehicle crashes related to drinking. It is likewise a safe assumption that drinkers who routinely lose consciousness or require emergency medical care are struggling with an alcohol problem. Tragically, such individuals may try to stop drinking but discover it is far more difficult to do so than they imagined it would be when they took their first sip.

THREE

GETTING WASTED AND WASTING AWAY

After a year of heavy drinking, fourteen-year-old Lynne arrived at an important realization when she stared into her mirror. Though still young, the North Carolina teen knew she wouldn't look that way forever if her alcohol abuse didn't come to an end. "I was afraid of what my reflection would show when I was eighteen," Lynne notes. "At the rate I was going, I knew that I'd look completely washed up by the time I turned twenty-one and could finally go to the liquor store to buy my own alcohol."

When Lynne finally reached this conclusion, she admits that alcohol abuse was already taking a brutal toll on her body. "I lost a ton of weight after I started drinking," she says. "I didn't have any appetite, and I drank to the point that I was always throwing up." Lynne also admits that she frequently experienced blackouts, lost consciousness, and risked her life on several occasions.

Unsurprisingly, this cycle of intoxication and illness eventually strained her mental health as well. "Drinking became both physically and emotioally exhausting," she recalls. "I lost friends because I was always drunk and obnoxious, and it gets depressing when you find yourself sitting alone in your room with a bottle. I was totally miserable, and the alcohol . . . began to mess with my head."

> "Drinking became both physically and emotionally exhausting. . . . [I]t gets depressing when you find yourself sitting alone in your room with a bottle." — Lynne

While Lynne insists that she never actively thought about suicide, she acknowledges that she had little drive to stop herself from wasting away. "I was heading to a place that, looking back, I wouldn't ever want to go now," she admits. "When I was drinking, though, I didn't care about myself—

ALCOHOL ABUSE

I only cared about the alcohol. Getting drunk feels good at first, but that's not what you end up experiencing when you finish the bottle and have to wake up the next day."

BEHAVIOR THAT POISONS THE BODY

Many people who abuse alcohol can relate to the physical and emotional side effects Lynne experienced. The impact alcohol abuse has on a person's body depends on several factors, including how long it has been occurring. Someone's overall health, as well as how much and how often the person drinks, also play important roles.

People whose alcohol abuse has developed into alcoholism tend to have a wider range of physical complications. But just because a person isn't a full-blown alcoholic doesn't mean that his or her problem won't ultimately prove deadly. Even someone who isn't dealing with physical addiction can easily die from alcohol poisoning after drinking too much in too short a period of time. Alcohol is a depressant that is rapidly absorbed into the bloodstream. Consuming large quantities of it can bring a drinker's bodily systems to a crashing halt.

A Significant Student Issue

Up until seventh grade, Lynne was enrolled in a local school. At that point, however, her mother began homeschooling her. According to Lynne, alcohol abuse took a toll on her abilities as a student in both environments. "Before I was homeschooled, I would often fall asleep during classes," she explains. "Drinking all the time really drains your motivation and focus, and my grades started slipping."

Lynne acknowledges that a shift to home-schooling didn't automatically improve her student career. "I continued to drink, and I was drinking heavily," she recalls. "As a result, I skipped most of the work I was supposed to be doing at home with my mom. I didn't really take it seriously."

ALCOHOL ABUSE

Nerves that control everything from breathing to the gag reflex to consciousness function more slowly—if they manage to function at all. Since heavy drinking frequently leads to stomach upset and vomiting, not being able to breathe and swallow normally can cause people to choke or suffocate if they throw up. Binge drinkers also suffer sudden drops in body temperature and blood sugar levels that can result in heart failure and **seizures**. It is not unusual for people with alcohol poisoning to require emergency medical treatment. Doctors often try to flush any remaining alcohol out of a patient's body by pumping, or suctioning, the contents of the stomach.

While many drinkers are affected by alcohol poisoning, it is not the only example of how alcohol abuse impacts physical health. Many people who have a drinking problem also experience blackouts. At the very least, most drinkers are familiar with the dizziness, blurred vision, slurred speech, poor coordination and reaction time, and subsequent hangovers that go hand-in-hand with being drunk. As their alcohol abuse progresses, a great number of individuals suffer from sleep disruptions, exhaustion, and appetite and weight changes as well.

Alcohol abuse takes a serious and sometimes deadly toll on a drinker's body.

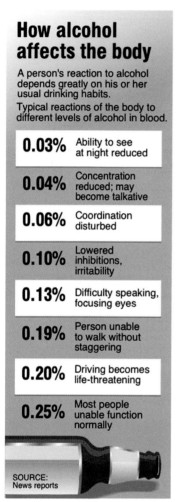

How alcohol affects the body

A person's reaction to alcohol depends greatly on his or her usual drinking habits.
Typical reactions of the body to different levels of alcohol in blood.

BAC	Reaction
0.03%	Ability to see at night reduced
0.04%	Concentration reduced; may become talkative
0.06%	Coordination disturbed
0.10%	Lowered inhibitions, irritability
0.13%	Difficulty speaking, focusing eyes
0.19%	Person unable to walk without staggering
0.20%	Driving becomes life-threatening
0.25%	Most people unable function normally

SOURCE:
News reports

If people don't take steps to curb their drinking, it is likely that they will be forced to cope with the long-term impacts of alcoholism. These include stomach **ulcers** and heart, kidney, and liver disease. Alcoholics also suffer an increased risk of being diagnosed with certain cancers and experiencing damage to their nervous systems.

HOW DRINKING DAMAGES THE MIND

The mental and emotional impacts of alcohol abuse can be just as devastating as any physical problems this condition triggers. In many situations, all

This chart explains the different effects that alcohol has on a person's body as his or her blood alcohol content (BAC) increases.

32

STARTLING STAT

THE **CDC** RECENTLY REPORTED THAT ROUGHLY 190,000 EMERGENCY-ROOM VISITS WERE MADE BY PEOPLE YOUNGER THAN TWENTY-ONE WHO WERE EITHER INJURED OR SICK AS A RESULT OF SITUATIONS INVOLVING ALCOHOL.

of these negative effects are strongly linked to one another. For instance, alcohol is known to alter brain chemicals that people rely on to control their impulses, reactions, and desires. Driving while drunk and having unprotected sex are consequently a few examples of how drinkers may respond to being intoxicated. People who abuse alcohol are therefore at greater risk of being involved in a car accident, getting pregnant, or catching a sexually transmitted disease (STD).

Such individuals also appear to be more likely to struggle with serious depression and anxiety. While researchers believe that these conditions can increase the risk that a person will abuse alcohol, they suspect that the opposite cause-and-effect relationship

Alcohol and College Students— A Dangerous Mix

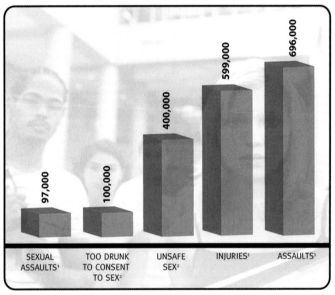

97,000	100,000	400,000	599,000	696,000
SEXUAL ASSAULTS[1]	TOO DRUNK TO CONSENT TO SEX[2]	UNSAFE SEX[2]	INJURIES[1]	ASSAULTS[1]

A graph from the National Institute on Alcohol Abuse and Alcoholism (NIAAA) profiles the frequency of certain problem behaviors connected to drinking.

occurs as well. This is because drinking impacts the brain chemicals that regulate people's moods and how they experience pleasure.

Many individuals who abuse alcohol also discover that they lose motivation and focus as drinking plays

STARTLING STAT

IN 2008, THE NATIONAL CENTER FOR HEALTH STATIS-
TICS (NCHS) ESTIMATED THAT ALCOHOL PLAYED A ROLE
IN ABOUT 30 PERCENT OF ALL SUICIDES.

an increasingly important role in their day-to-day lives. Depending on how severe their abuse is, they may feel that it is difficult to concentrate or fulfill their responsibilities without having a drink or getting drunk. In fact, the frustration, depression, and anxiety that people with a drinking problem face can be so overwhelming that they become suicidal. Yet the destruction that results from alcohol abuse doesn't simply hurt whoever is lifting a bottle to their lips. The impacts of this issue lead to turmoil and tragedy for countless friends and family members as well.

FOUR

HOW ALCOHOL AFFECTS RELATIONSHIPS

EIGHTEEN-YEAR-OLD KYLE ADMITS that he "really didn't care about anyone or anything" when he was drinking. He specifically recalls having little interest in obeying his parents' rules or treating them with respect during this period in his life—especially if he was busy partying. The California teen also painfully recalls how alcohol jeopardized his relationship with his mother on one especially memorable summer afternoon in 2009.

Though Kyle says he wasn't drunk, he confesses that he had been drinking earlier in the day. Yet he soon realized that he had to drive himself to an alcohol- and substance-abuse education meeting—with his mother in the passenger's seat. Kyle ultimately made the decision to turn the keys in the ignition with her at his side.

Luckily for both of them, they arrived at the program site safely, but he failed a required Breathalyzer test shortly thereafter. Not only did the results of the test lead to Kyle getting kicked out of the program, it also had a painful impact on his relationship with his mother.

"My mom was pretty hurt and upset when she learned that I had been drinking and that I had driven us there anyway," he says. "I love my mom. I would never want to do anything that would put her in any kind of danger, but I did." Nor was Kyle's mother

---

"My mom was pretty hurt and upset when she learned that I had been drinking and that I had driven us . . . anyway. I love my mom. I would never want to do anything that would put her in any kind of danger, but I did." —Kyle

"I lost friends over some of the things I did when I was drunk." — Kyle

the only person to be negatively affected by his drinking.

His problems with alcohol took a similarly destructive toll on his relationships with peers. "I lost friends over some of the things I did when I was drunk," Kyle reflects. "I hated school and was always fighting everyone. Now I can see that I was really just scared."

MORE THAN A ONE-PERSON PROBLEM

Since alcohol abuse alters drinkers' physical and mental health, this problem inevitably affects their family members and friends, as well. Everyone from parents and teachers to siblings and peers are frequently hurt and confused by the behavioral changes they observe in people with a drinking problem.

In certain cases, such individuals start demonstrating a variety of negative behaviors that take a toll on their personal relationships. These include breaking rules and treating adults with disrespect and defiance. People with a drinking problem may also become less responsible and reliable at home, school, and work. Some even develop a reputation in their

Another Person's Point of View

Twenty-nine-year-old Josh says that he and Kyle are "basically like brothers." Yet he also acknowledges that Kyle's drinking problem "drove a huge wedge" into their relationship. Even though they have known each other for about twelve years, Josh emphasizes that alcohol ultimately put that bond to the test.

"It was super difficult to watch him self-destruct and spiral downward because of alcohol," he remarks. "[Since he got treatment] he's [become] a much more mature person for having owned up to his problems and for having worked to overcome them."

When asked what recommendations he has for friends and family who are trying to support someone experiencing alcohol abuse, Josh offers the following tip: "Remember that recovery is about progress—not perfection. It is a process, and it won't happen immediately. Keep this in mind, and don't get frustrated!"

People who abuse alcohol often turn away from friends and loved ones who express concern about their behavior.

communities for committing crimes while drunk. Driving under the influence of alcohol, vandalism, theft, and assault are just a few examples of criminal activities that have been linked to underage drinking.

Individuals who abuse alcohol don't have to be found guilty of a crime for their problem to impact the people around them. For instance, many gradually spend less and less time with friends and family members. They instead seek out the company of acquaintances who can either obtain alcohol for them or who have a reputation for drinking or doing drugs.

In addition, people who abuse alcohol often become more physically and emotionally aggressive. This behavior may be most apparent when they are drinking or intoxicated. Such drinkers might seem

A common sign of alcohol abuse is aggression toward others.

> **"Alcohol abuse is highly toxic to personal relationships. . . . In a lot of cases, [friends and family members are] dealing with someone who's got a 'whatever' attitude about pretty much everything besides alcohol."**
> **— Brian Bossany**

unusually hostile, defensive, or eager to pick fights. Some go so far as to become physically or verbally abusive to friends and family members.

"Alcohol abuse is highly toxic to personal relationships," observes Brian Bossany. "It leads to stress and increased arguments and can leave friends and family members feeling completely helpless. In a lot of cases, they're dealing with someone who's got a 'whatever' attitude about pretty much everything besides alcohol."

STARTLING STAT

THE WISCONSIN COALITION AGAINST SEXUAL ASSAULT (WCASA) REVEALED THAT ALCOHOL PLAYED A ROLE IN MORE THAN 50 PERCENT OF CASES INVOLVING DATE RAPE OR ACQUAINTANCE RAPE.

WHY HEALING HAPPENS SLOWLY

When people finally acknowledge their alcohol abuse and seek treatment, they take the first steps toward improving both their lives and those of everyone who cares about them. Nevertheless, evaluating what triggered and enabled people's alcohol abuse can be as painful and challenging a process for family and friends as it is for drinkers themselves.

Part of getting and staying sober involves coming to terms with how a person's drinking hurts others.

Recovery involves a former drinker taking responsibility for his or her behavior while abusing alcohol.

Since people with a drinking problem frequently suffer memory lapses and blackouts, hearing about how they acted when they were intoxicated can be an embarrassing, emotional experience. On the other hand, discussing and reliving such events can be equally difficult for friends and family members.

In addition, it is not unusual for parents and peers to have intense feelings of guilt and denial as they watch someone they love fight to achieve sobriety. Many friends and family members blame themselves for not perceiving the person's drinking problem sooner or for not doing more to actively end it. Others may not struggle with these emotions as much as they do with the overall challenge of learning how to

STARTLING STAT

A 2010 STUDY CONDUCTED BY THE MAINE OFFICE OF SUBSTANCE ABUSE REVEALED THAT LESS THAN 2 PERCENT OF PARENTS THOUGHT THEIR TEENAGER HAD EVER EXPERIENCED AN EPISODE OF BINGE DRINKING. IN REALITY, MORE THAN 20 PERCENT OF THE TEENS SURVEYED ADMITTED TO THIS TYPE OF BEHAVIOR.

forgive someone who has hurt or betrayed them by abusing alcohol.

Most people who have experienced a drinking problem ultimately discover that it takes time and effort to reestablish relationships that are built on honesty and trust. Meanwhile, many also face new challenges in their interactions with peers. Someone who is working to maintain sobriety must frequently make difficult choices about who his or her real friends are.

Those peers who support a person's sobriety will inevitably suggest activities that don't involve alcohol. Yet certain friends and acquaintances may not fully understand or appreciate someone's drinking problem. People attempting to overcome alcohol abuse must therefore think carefully about which of their relationships are helpful—and which are potentially harmful—to their continued recovery.

FIVE

A REALISTIC LOOK AT RECOVERY

FOR EIGHTEEN-YEAR-OLD EMILY, RECOVERY has been a long and sometimes frustrating process. She remembers first drinking at the age of thirteen, though it took her several more years to recognize that she abused alcohol.

Emily's turning point in her battle with alcohol abuse came on November 28, 2010. The Minnesota teen and some of her friends decided to get drunk at an acquaintance's house. Much of what occurred that evening is a blur, but Emily has since learned that other partygoers took all the money she had been carrying with her. As she attempted to walk home with a friend, she slipped and fell on an icy road, where she was essentially left to die. Fortunately, police eventually rescued her, though they and doctors informed her that, given her condition and the bitter winter weather, she was extremely lucky to have survived.

"That was the moment that really convinced me that I needed to stop once and for all," emphasizes Emily. "I have recently started going to Alcoholics Anonymous (AA) meetings one to two times per week, and I'm enrolled at Sobriety High." Attending a charter school that both supports her recovery and allows her to earn her diploma is a huge benefit to Emily, who states that she probably wouldn't otherwise be able to graduate.

"I understand certain things now that I didn't when I first began treatment," she says. "I know that no normal person drinks every day, all day—like I was doing in the past. I have accepted that I can't have even a single drink if I truly want to make it."

"I understand certain things now that I didn't when I first began treatment. . . . I have accepted that I can't have even a single drink if I truly want to make it." — Emily

---

STARTLING STAT

IN 2009 RESEARCHERS WITH THE NATIONAL INSTITUTE ON DRUG ABUSE (NIDA) INDICATED THAT ONLY ABOUT 11 PERCENT OF AMERICANS AGES TWELVE AND OLDER WHO ARE SUFFERING FROM SUBSTANCE ABUSE OR ADDICTION ARE RECEIVING TREATMENT.

AN INDIVIDUALIZED PROCESS

Before people who abuse alcohol make the decision to work toward rehabilitation—or treatment and recovery—most usually reach a turning point in their battle with alcohol. This might be a near-death experience or a brush with law enforcement. In other cases, it's the realization that drinking is taking a heavy toll on their health and personal relationships.

No matter what triggers this turning point, it sometimes results in drinkers admitting to their alcohol abuse and independently asking for help. In certain situations, however, a person's drinking problem becomes so obvious that the people around that individual stage an **intervention.** Everyone from his or her friends and family members to counselors and

Interventions are meant to encourage people to get help. They should not be about making drinkers feel ashamed or embarrassed.

doctors who are trained to deal with alcohol abuse may be present at an intervention. They typically confront the drinker about the problem and either ask or insist that the person get treatment. Regardless of what ultimately encourages a person to seek help, Claudia Welke explains that what happens next depends on a variety of factors.

"Treatment is a very individualized process," she notes. "How long [someone] has been abusing alcohol, the intensity of their abuse, and what the

"Treatment is a very individualized process. How long [someone] has been abusing alcohol, the intensity of their abuse, and what the risks or consequences of their drinking have been are all considerations."
— Claudia Welke, MD

risks or consequences of their drinking have been are all considerations." While health-care providers and parents often play an important role in determining a treatment strategy, most experts advise that patients also be given a voice during planning. Luckily, people today have a wide range of choices when it comes to programs that are designed to help them get and stay sober.

Residential and inpatient facilities generally involve patients staying at a hospital or an off-site treatment center for anywhere from seven to thirty days. These programs are frequently the best options for people who are struggling with alcoholism or severe alcohol abuse. Patients who fit this description sometimes need to undergo **detoxification**, or detox, before they begin treatment. During detox, heavy drinkers experience various physical and emotional withdrawal symptoms as their bodies grow accustomed to the absence of alcohol. Inpatient or residential programs are also a good fit for patients whose home environments put them at immediate risk of relapsing. In addition, they tend to be more effective for people dealing with other comorbid conditions, such as depression, anxiety, or drug addiction.

Yet not everyone working to overcome alcohol abuse decides to participate in an inpatient treatment program. Outpatient care is an option for people who

Counselors are trained to guide former drinkers through the recovery process.

are in the early stages of a drinking problem or who do not drink on a daily basis. Most outpatient treatment lasts anywhere from one to twelve months. Ideally, individuals who choose an outpatient plan are not at immediate risk of jeopardizing their own safety or that of the people around them. In the majority of cases, they live at home and continue attending school. They generally visit a hospital, medical office, or treatment center for routine counseling sessions.

FROM COUNSELING TO AFTERCARE

Regardless of the different strategies people use to tackle alcohol abuse, many treatment plans share a few common features. For example, a great number of recovery programs include **psychotherapy**, or "talk therapy," with a trained therapist, counselor, psychologist, or psychiatrist. Individuals who participate in psychotherapy explore what triggered their drinking problem and discuss how alcohol abuse has negatively affected their lives and relationships.

This counseling is often only part of people's strategy to get and stay sober. People who have a history of alcohol abuse face a future that is inevitably filled with temptation and uncertainty. This is why it

Reflections and Realizations

William and Sandra are no strangers to the devastating effects of alcohol abuse. Both in their forties, the North Carolina couple are also the parents of two children—ages fourteen and twenty—who have struggled with similar issues. Though their family has experienced a tremendous amount of pain and hardship, both husband and wife have learned several invaluable lessons as a result of their battle with alcohol.

"My advice to [people] who suspect that they may have a drinking problem is to talk to someone as soon as possible," recommends Sandra. "If you can't reach out to a friend or family member, go to an AA meeting. If you don't have transportation, find a group or a meeting online."

William, who has been sober for twenty years, has a few additional words of wisdom. "If you're struggling to overcome alcohol abuse, remember that your problem didn't happen overnight," he says. "The cure won't happen overnight either. Bear in mind that there is a silver lining to your situation, though. I'm happier now that I'm sober than I ever was before. I'm finally comfortable being who I am without alcohol."

is so important for them to work with friends, family members, counselors, and medical professionals to develop a long-term sobriety plan. Patients' efforts to maintain an alcohol-free lifestyle following treatment are commonly referred to as aftercare.

For those who have previously abused alcohol, efforts to avoid relapse frequently consist of attending support-group meetings. Several support groups, including AA, encourage former drinkers to maintain

A counselor outlines a twelve-step plan at an AA meeting.

STARTLING STAT

A RECENT STUDY BY **SAMHSA** SHOWED THAT
ROUGHLY 56 PERCENT OF SUBSTANCE-ABUSE TREATMENT
FACILITIES ALWAYS OR OFTEN RELIED ON TWELVE-STEP
PROGRAMMING.

day-to-day sobriety by following a twelve-step plan.
This strategy typically features a dozen principles or
traditions that people are advised to reflect on and
put into action in their lives. The steps are supposed
to help people achieve physical, mental, emotional,
and sometimes spiritual recovery.

In addition to relying on a twelve-step plan, many
individuals who are recovering from a drinking problem stay sober by routinely communicating with a
sponsor. Sponsors are mentors who are further along
in their recovery. These men and women volunteer to
use their experiences to guide other people as they
push beyond a past that involves alcohol abuse.

SIX

ANSWERS TO ALCOHOL ABUSE

MOST INDIVIDUALS WHO HAVE EXPE-rienced alcohol abuse understand that there's no silver-bullet solution that will make this issue disappear. People like Lynne have a few ideas about what society could do to help the public better understand the realities of the problem. "I think it would make a difference for the media to show what alcohol abuse actually does to a person," the North Carolina teen notes. "People living with this problem don't have steady jobs. They put themselves at risk of getting robbed or hurt when they're drunk all the time. It's important for kids to see those realities."

> "I think it would make a difference for the media to show what alcohol abuse actually does to a person. . . . It's important for kids to see those realities."— Lynne

Claudia Welke agrees that instead of revealing the facts about alcohol abuse, the media frequently glamorizes drinking. "If you pay attention to the lyrics of certain songs by popular musicians, you hear what almost sounds like a glorification of getting drunk and doing drugs," she explains. "I think that kids really do look up to celebrities and performers

STARTLING STAT

THE FEDERAL TRADE COMMISSION (FTC) INDICATED THAT MAGAZINES AIMED AT AUDIENCES YOUNGER THAN TWENTY-ONE CONTAINED 92 PERCENT MORE ADS FOR ALCOHOLIC BEVERAGES THAN DID PUBLICATIONS TARGETING OLDER READERS.

Singer/songwriter Amy Winehouse was one of many celebrities who publicly battled alcohol abuse.

and listen to what they say. It would therefore be good if the media remembered that fact in the messages it sends about alcohol."

THE RESPONSIBILITY OF ROLE MODELS

Eighteen-year-old Emily supports Welke's and Lynne's opinions. Yet she also notes that education about the dangers of drinking largely begins at home. "Parents and older siblings need to understand that they are huge role models," says the Minnesota teen. "Their actions set an example for younger people. Their alcohol use or attitudes about alcohol send a message to teenagers."

To this end, Emily offers the following tips to parents: "Keep kids in check. Don't allow them to feel like underage drinking will result in a lesser punishment than doing drugs. Finally, it's honestly not a bad idea to consider putting a lock on your liquor cabinet."

> "Parents and older siblings need to understand that they are huge role models. Their actions set an example for younger people. Their alcohol use or attitudes about alcohol send a message to teenagers."
> — Emily

59

STARTLING STAT

BASED ON RESEARCH CONDUCTED BETWEEN 2006 AND 2009 BY THE U.S. DEPARTMENT OF HEALTH AND HUMAN SERVICES, ABOUT 45 PERCENT OF TWELVE- TO FOURTEEN-YEAR-OLD DRINKERS OBTAINED ALCOHOL FROM FAMILY MEMBERS OR FROM WITHIN THEIR OWN HOMES.

MORE OPPORTUNITIES FOR ACCEPTANCE

Like Emily, eighteen-year-old Kyle grasps the role that parents play when it comes to preventing and overcoming alcohol abuse. At the same time, however, the California teen is quick to emphasize that it's important for adults to do more than patrol their kids and stage interventions. From his perspective, one effective approach to tackling alcohol abuse is to offer people more opportunities to connect, communicate, and feel accepted.

"Kids need to have someone that they can talk to and trust," he says. "They want to be able to turn to someone who they know will love them—no matter

Support from friends and family is an important element in the recovery process.

"Kids need to have someone that they can talk to and trust. They want to be able to turn to someone who they know will love them—no matter what problems they're dealing with." — Kyle

what problems they're dealing with." Yet, as Kyle acknowledges, finding people—whether they're parents or peers—who provide unconditional support and accept-ance is not always a simple task. Nevertheless, he believes that it's a critical part of achieving and maintaining sobriety.

"I'm currently involved in a Christian outreach program called Young Life," he says. "I hope to lock into something similar when I start college. I feel it will help me stay sober because the people I've met through the program offer love and encouragement regardless of how you come to them. That's a huge thing for kids who are trying to work past alcohol [abuse]."

As Kyle, Emily, and Lynne are the first to admit, such individuals will likely face a bumpy, unpredictable road as they attempt to overcome their problems.

Yet these three people are also living proof that, despite the darkness and danger that go hand-in-hand with alcohol abuse, the future can be far brighter than the past. By sharing their experiences, opinions, and ideas, they are taking a powerful stand against a troubling teen issue.

Show Your Support!

April is Alcohol Awareness Month, and September is National Recovery Month. See if your school or community leaders can arrange guest speakers, group discussions, and other special programming to help educate people about alcohol abuse. Alternately, consider posting or distributing fliers that provide information about the warning signs of a drinking problem, as well as local treatment resources.

Status Update on Teen Sources

LYNNE reported that she was making progress in her studies as a home-schooled student. She was grateful for the ongoing support of her parents, who have also battled alcohol abuse, in her own recovery efforts.

KYLE said he was doing great. After participating in a successful treatment program, he was enjoying his new outlook on life and was spending much of his time playing music, attending classes, and working at a coffee shop and as a youth counselor.

EMILY indicated that she was continuing her education at Sobriety High in Minnesota. She explained that she had finally reached a point where she recognized the severity of her problem and was committed to achieving and maintaining a totally alcohol-free future.

Notes

CHAPTER 1

p. 5, "According to a 2010 . . .": statistical data on the
    prevalence of drinking among eighth graders,
    "Prevalence of Underage Drinking," Johns Hopkins
    Bloomberg School of Public Health, 24 October
    2011, www.camy.org/factsheets/sheets/Prevalence_of_
    Underage_Drinking.html.

p. 6, "I drank to get drunk . . .": Lynne*. Personal interview.
    27 March 2011.

p. 6, "I drank until I . . .": Lynne. Personal interview.
    27 March 2011.

p. 7, "It's all about finding . . .": Lynne. Personal interview.
    27 March 2011.

p. 7, "*Alcoholism* occurs when a person . . .": verbiage
    of definitions of "alcoholism" and "alcohol abuse,"
    "Alcoholism and Alcohol Abuse," the National Institutes
    of Health (NIH), 28 March 2011, www.nlm.nih.gov/
    medlineplus/ency/article/000944.htm.

p. 10, "For a person who abuses . . .": Bossany, Brian. Personal
    interview. 16 March 2011.

p. 10, "safe, sober, and chemical-free environment": verbiage
    describing Sobriety High, "Sobriety High Charter
    School," Sobriety High, 12 December 2010, www.
    sobrietyhighschool.com.

p. 10, "I hear . . . a lot . . .": Bossany, Brian. Personal interview.
    16 March 2011.

p. 10, "In 2010 the Centers for . . .": statistical data on the
    prevalence high school students who binge drink, "CDC
    Report: One in Four High-School Students and Young
    Adults Admit to Binge Drinking," *ISHN Magazine*, 9

October 2010, www.ishn.com/articles/print/90309html.

p. 13, "In 2009 the Substance Abuse ..." statistical data on the prevalence of underage drinking in the United States, "Adults Encourage Underage Drinking," The National Family Partnership (NFP), 3 December 2009, www.nfp.org/default.asp?PageNum=741.

p. 13, "Not all of these ..." statistical data on the number of underage drinkers who abuse alcohol, "Adults Encourage Underage Drinking," the NFP, 3 December 2009, www.nfp.org/default.asp?PageNum=741.

p. 13, "Among youth, ... alcohol and other ...": verbiage describing the effects of adolescent alcohol abuse, "Alcohol and Drug Use," the Centers for Disease Control and Prevention (CDC), 3 June 2010, www.cdc.gov/healthyyouth/alcoholdrug/index.htm.

p. 15, "I'm seeing [patients] who are ...": Welke, Claudia. Personal interview. 27 March 2011.

p. 15, "[People] whose parents routinely ...": Welke, Claudia. Personal interview. 27 March 2011.

CHAPTER 2

p. 16, "pretty much a really ...": Kyle. Personal interview. 22 March 2011.

p. 17, "2011 CBS News ...": statistical data on the percentage of Americans who try drinking before they finish high school, "Teenage Drug Abuse Skyrockets," CBS News, 6 April 2011, www.cbsnews.com/stories/2011/04/06/eveningnews/main20051485.shtml.

p. 17, "I wouldn't describe myself ...": Kyle. Personal interview. 22 March 2011.

p. 18, "My perspective has definitely ...": Kyle. Personal interview. 22 March 2011.

p. 20, "The National Survey on . . .": statistical data on the percentage of severely depressed teens who had recently used alcohol, "Results from the 2008 National Survey on Drug Use and Health (NSDUH): National Findings," The U.S. Department of Health and Human Services (SAMHSA), September 2009, www.oas.samhsa.gov/nsduh/2k8nsduh/2k8Results.cfm#8.2.2.

p. 24, "The physical red flags aren't. . .": Welke, Claudia. Personal interview. 27 March 2011.

CHAPTER 3

p. 26, "I was afraid of what . . .": Lynne. Personal interview. 27 March 2011.

p. 26, "I lost a ton . . .": Lynne. Personal interview. 27 March 2011.

p. 27, "Drinking became both physically and . . .": Lynne. Personal interview. 27 March 2011.

p. 27, "I was heading to a place . . .": Lynne. Personal interview. 27 March 2011.

p. 29, "Before I was homeschooled . . .": Lynne. Personal interview. 7 April 2011.

p. 29, "I continued to drink . . .": Lynne. Personal interview. 7 April 2011.

p. 33, "In 2008 the CDC . . .": statistical data on the percentage of people under twenty-one hospitalized for alcohol-related injuries and illnesses, "Fact Sheets: Underage Drinking," the CDC, 20 July 2010, www.cdc.gov/alcohol/fact-sheets/underage-drinking.htm.

p. 35, "In 2008 the National . . .": statistical data on the percentage of suicides in which alcohol was a factor, "Facts and Figures: National Statistics," the American Foundation for Suicide Prevention (AFSP), (specific date

last updated not available) 2011, www.afsp.org/index.
cfm?fuseaction=home.viewpage&page_id=050fea9f-
b064-4092-b1135c3a70de1fda.

CHAPTER 4

p. 36, "really didn't care about anyone . . .": Kyle. Personal
interview. 22 March 2011.

p. 37, "My mom was pretty hurt . . .": Kyle. Personal interview.
22 March 2011.

p. 38, "I lost friends over some . . .": Kyle. Personal interview.
22 March 2011.

p. 39, "basically like brothers": Josh. Personal interview.
8 April 2011.

p. 39, "drove a huge wedge": Josh. Personal interview.
8 April 2011.

p. 39, "It was super difficult . . . .": Josh. Personal interview.
8 April 2011.

p. 39, "Remember that recovery is . . .": Josh. Personal
interview. 8 April 2011.

p. 42, "Alcohol abuse is highly toxic . . .": Bossany, Brian.
Personal interview. 16 March 2011.

p. 42, "In 2008 the Wisconsin . . .": statistical data on the
percentage of date rapes and acquaintance rapes that
involve alcohol, "Campus Sexual Assaults," the University
of Wisconsin–Oshkosh, 10 May 2011, www.uwosh.edu/
cvpp/sexual-assault/campus-sexual-assault-statistics.

p. 44, "A 2010 study conducted . . .": statistical data on the
percentage of parents who incorrectly assume that their
teens never binge drink, "Teens and Drinking," *The Bangor
Daily News*, 12 September 2010, www.bangordailynews.
com/2010/09/12/opinion/teens-and-drinking.

CHAPTER 5

p. 47, "That was the moment that . . .": Emily. Personal interview. 5 April 2011.

p. 47, "I understand certain things . . .": Emily. Personal interview. 5 April 2011.

p. 47, "In 2009 researchers with . . .": statistical data on the percentage of Americans ages twelve or older who receive treatment for their substance abuse/addiction, "The National Institute on Drug Abuse (NIDA): InfoFacts: Treatment Statistics," the NIDA, March 2011, www.nida.nih.gov/infofacts/treatmenttrends.html.

p. 49, "Treatment is a very individualized . . .": Welke, Claudia. Personal interview. 27 March 2011.

p. 53, "My advice to [people] . . .": Sandra. Personal interview. 5 April 2011.

p. 53, "If you're struggling to . . .": William. Personal interview. 5 April 2011.

p. 53, "A study conducted in 2009 . . .": statistical data on the percentage of substance-abuse treatment facilities that use twelve-step programming, "Clinical or Therapeutic Approaches Used by Substance Abuse Treatment Facilities," the SAMHSA, 14 October 2010, www.oas.samhsa.gov/2k10/238/238ClinicalAp2k10.htm.

CHAPTER 6

p. 56, "I think it would make . . .": Lynne. Personal interview. 27 March 2011.

p. 57, "If you pay attention . . .": Welke, Claudia. Personal interview. 27 March 2011.

p. 57, "A 2008 report by . . .": statistical data on the percentage of alcohol ads in magazines for readers younger than twenty-one, "Helping Youth Unravel Media Messages," StopAlcoholAbuse.gov, (specific date last updated not

available), www.stopalcoholabuse.gov/townhallmeetings/
article_helpingyouth.aspx.

p. 59, "Parents and older siblings . . .": Emily. Personal
interview. 5 April 2011.

p. 59, "Keep kids in check. Don't . . .": Emily. Personal
interview. 5 April 2011.

p. 60, "Based on research conducted . . .": statistical data on
how twelve- to fourteen-year-old drinkers obtain their
alcohol, "Most Kids Who Drink Get Alcohol from
Family," MSNBC, 17 February 2011, www.msnbc.msn.
com/id/41647460/ns/health-addictions/t/most-kids-who-
drink-get-alcohol-family.

p. 60, "Kids need to have . . .": Kyle. Personal interview.
22 March 2011.

p. 62, "I'm currently involved in . . .": Kyle. Personal interview.
22 March 2011.

Glossary

Alcoholics Anonymous (AA) a well-known network of support groups that operate with the purpose of helping people overcome alcohol abuse and addiction

Breathalyzer a device that is used to measure the amount of alcohol present in a person's blood

comorbid diseases or medical conditions that occur in a patient at about the same time

detoxification the process by which a person stops drinking and remains sober until there are no longer any traces of alcohol in his or her body

hangover unpleasant aftereffects that result from consuming too much alcohol

intervention a meeting in which people confront someone they know about his or her substance abuse in the hopes of providing that person with help

intoxicated so affected by drugs or alcohol that someone's physical and emotional perceptions and responses become altered

peers people who share equal standing with
others in a larger group

psychotherapy treatment for mental or
emotional conditions that relies on
communication with a therapist

relapsing returning to undesirable behavior

seizures symptoms of abnormal brain activity
that often involve shaking, trembling, or a loss
of consciousness

sober not affected by chemical substances such as
drugs and alcohol

traumatic emotionally or physically shocking

ulcers breaks in the tissue lining of the stomach

Further Information

BOOKS

Burlingame, Jeff. *Alcohol*. New York: Cavendish Square
    Publishing, LLC, 2014.

Lily, Henrietta M. *Frequently Asked Questions about
    Alcohol Abuse and Binge Drinking*. New York: Rosen
    Publishing, 2012.

Rooney, Anne. *Alcohol*. Mankato, MN: Arcturus
    Publishing, 2011.

Stewart, Gail B. *Drowning in a Bottle: Teens and Alcohol
    Abuse*. Mankato, MN: Compass Point Books, 2009.

WEBSITES

The Cool Spot—Too Much, Too Soon, Too Risky

www.thecoolspot.gov/too_much.asp

A website sponsored by the National Institute on
Alcohol Abuse and Alcoholism (NIAAA) that offers
quizzes, statistics, and other fast facts on underage
drinking and peer pressure.

TeensHealth—Drugs and Alcohol

www.kidshealth.org/teen/drug_alcohol/

A website that provides data on alcohol, as well as
what to do if you or someone you know might have a
problem with it.

Bibliography

BOOKS

Bradley, Michael. *When Things Get Crazy with Your Teen: The Why, the How, and What to Do Now.* New York: McGraw-Hill, 2009.

Edvin, David, and Samuel Harald (editors). *Underage Drinking: Examining and Preventing Youth Use of Alcohol.* New York: Nova Science Publishers, 2010.

Inciardi, James, and Karen McElrath (editors). *The American Drug Scene: An Anthology.* New York: Oxford University Press, 2008.

Lebow, Jay L. *Handbook of Clinical Family Therapy.* Hoboken, NJ: John Wiley, 2005.

Winters, Ken C. (editor). *Adolescent Substance Abuse: New Frontiers in Assessment.* New York: The Haworth Press, 2006.

Yoshida, Rin (editor). *Trends in Alcohol Abuse and Alcoholism Research.* New York: Nova Science Publishers, 2007.

ONLINE ARTICLES

"Adults Encourage Underage Drinking," the National Family Partnership (NFP), 3 December 2009, www.nfp.org/default.asp?PageNum=741.

"Alcohol and Drug Use," the Centers for Disease Control and Prevention (CDC), 3 June 2010, www.cdc.gov/healthyyouth/alcoholdrug/index.htm.

"Alcoholism and Alcohol Abuse," the National Institutes of Health (NIH), 28 March 2011, www.nlm.nih.gov/medlineplus/ency/article/000944.htm.

"Campus Sexual Assaults," the University of Wisconsin–Oshkosh, 10 May 2011, www.uwosh.edu/cvpp/sexual-assault/campus-sexual-assault-statistics.

"CDC Report: One in Four High-School Students and Young Adults Admit to Binge Drinking," *ISHN Magazine*, 9 October 2010, www.ishn.com/articles/print/90309html.

"Clinical or Therapeutic Approaches Used by Substance Abuse Treatment Facilities," the U.S. Department of Health and Human Services (SAMHSA), 14 October 2010, www.oas.samhsa.gov/2k10/238/238ClinicalAp2k10.htm.

"Fact Sheets: Underage Drinking," the Centers for Disease Control and Prevention, 20 July 2010, www.cdc.gov/alcohol/fact-sheets/underage-drinking.htm.

"Facts and Figures: National Statistics," the American Foundation for Suicide Prevention (AFSP), (specific date last updated not available) 2011, www.afsp.org/index.cfm?fuseaction=home.viewpage&page_id=050fea9f-b064-4092-b1135c3a70de1fda.

"Helping Youth Unravel Media Messages," StopAlcoholAbuse.gov, (specific date last updated not available), www.stopalcoholabuse.gov/townhallmeetings/article_helpingyouth.aspx.

"Most Kids Who Drink Get Alcohol from Family," MSNBC, 17 February 2011, www.msnbc.msn.com/id/41647460/ns/health-addictions/t/most-kids-who-drink-get-alcohol-family/ .

"Prevalence of Underage Drinking," Johns Hopkins Bloomberg School of Public Health, 24 October 2011, www.camy.org/factsheets/sheets/Prevalence_of_Underage_Drinking.html.

"Results from the 2008 National Survey on Drug Use and Health (NSDUH): National Findings," the SAMHSA, September 2009, www.oas.samhsa.gov/nsduh/2k8nsduh/2k8Results.cfm#8.2.2.

"Sobriety High Charter School," Sobriety High, 12 December 2010, www.sobrietyhighschool.com.

"Teenage Drug Abuse Skyrockets," CBS News, 6 April 2011, www.cbsnews.com/stories/2011/04/06/eveningnews/main20051485.shtml.

"Teens and Drinking," *The Bangor Daily News*, 12 September 2010, www.bangordailynews.com/2010/09/12/opinion/teens-and-drinking.

"The National Institute on Drug Abuse (NIDA): InfoFacts: Treatment Statistics," the NIDA, March 2011, www.nida.nih.gov/infofacts/treatmenttrends.html.

PERSONAL INTERVIEWS

Brian Bossany (March 16, 2011)

Claudia Welke, MD (March 27, 2011)

Emily (April 5, 2011)

Josh (April 8, 2011)

Kyle (March 22, 2011; April 5, 2011)

Lynne* (March 27, 2011; April 7, 2011)

Sandra (April 5, 2011)

William (April 5, 2011)

Index

Page numbers in **boldface** are illustrations.

About the Author

KATIE MARSICO has authored more than eighty books for children and young adults. She lives in Elmhurst, Illinois, with her husband and children.